I0483532

Business Management in America my entrepreneurial perspective

By

Tonya B. Hunter

- **ISBN-10:** 1516809580
- **ISBN-13:** 978-1516809585

Dedication/acknowledgements

To all aspiring and future entrepreneurs.

CONTENTS

Introduction---

I am honored to be an entrepreneur who is able to pursue and follow my vision and developed my businesses from start-up. My work, education, and experiences over the past two decades has rendered me proficient knowledge and skills to perform in all aspects of the Healthcare Industry including direct patient care, Long-Term HealthCare, and insurance billing. I possess professional knowledge in all aspects of the business. I am known by the clients I serve, as well as my colleagues, as a consummate businessperson with-whom demonstrates personal integrity. I am known for my contagious, and excited desire for quality in business solutions, exceptional communication, and persuasive presentation that has led to profitable negotiations.

This book is in no way academic, even though I referenced some academic sources in my research. It is based on hard work, my perception, and my experiences with corporate America.

This book contains information that I have learned along the way and is still learning. This reading encompasses the basic facets of a business, becoming an entrepreneur, identifying services can offer or a problem that I can solve, assessing that service or problem to determine its value, establishing a brand, finding a location, obtaining zoning & licensures, funding the business idea, hiring staff, purchasing equipment and furniture, and finally determining a workable marketing strategy. Unequivocally understanding that managing a Health & Wellness Center is far different than managing other types of business.

Owning a Business

Introduction to business & entrepreneurship

What is a business? A business is where people work or what they do to sell services, goods or products. Sometimes these services are sold or exchanged for more services or sold and exchanged for money. The word business comes from the word busy with means occupied (Wikipedia). A business owner is the person who hires the people to work in the business. A business can be big, or it can be small. For example, you can become the owner of your own small company like a flower shop. Leaf raking can be a business, as well as owning a large company similar to that of Microsoft can be a business. What is entrepreneurship? Entrepreneurship is starting your business from the ground up. More than 70% of all small business have a single owner. Most businesses were created for commerce, but all businesses are good for the economy, especially small businesses.

Small businesses help the economy. There are more than 28 million small businesses in America. There are seven women to every ten men entrepreneurs. More than 16% of first generation immigrants started or ran startups in 2012, higher than the 13% participation rate for Americans who are not immigrants (Forbes).

Some regions of the United States rely heavily on small businesses. These regions include states like Montana and Wyoming. More than 50% of small businesses are home-based businesses. Small businesses, however sometimes have to compete with larger companies. It can be difficult because larger companies have the resources to squeeze small businesses out. It is sad when a big business makes it difficult for a smaller business to survive. Big business can hurt small business when they hoard money or keep a large amount of cash. A Small business may need to borrow money to stay afloat, and that money is needed for the economy to remain active. Some big businesses will hold on their money, not lending to small companies because they may see them as a risk in several aspects. They may see them as a risk of instability and unsustainability. Or they may see them as a risk as future competition. Things that affect small businesses are other small business, larger businesses, the use of the media, globalization and trade.

Business ethics is tremendously essential for an organization to be successful. It is important for a business to partake a progressive impression on the community in which it is operating. Ethics is defined as "study and philosophy of human conduct with an emphasis in determining the right and wrong." Organizations often face ethical quandaries in their

12

daily operation. A larger company may not see their actions as unethical, but as a reaction to remain profitable.

Every company wants to make huge profits. Profits are needed in order for a company to hire more staff, satisfy their investors and give back to the community. Often time companies get too involved in making money that they forget how to treat their employees. A company can improve the image of their brand by putting more emphasis on human beings and people. They can show employee appreciations by placing value on the employees.

The government creates laws that allow people to get rich, take advantage of loopholes, and use tax deductions then in turn punish them for the very success the government, afforded them. Wealth and success is obtained through hard work, sacrifices, and dedication. The reward for their hard work is sometimes monetary. A person should be allowed to do what they want with their money, and they are not obligated to share any of it. People should not feel guilty about acquiring wealth unless that wealth was obtained illegally or unethically. I do agree, however, that money causes harm when left to people who are unprepared.

Women in the workplace-

Women-owned businesses has increased over the last few years. Women-owned businesses has increased 68% over the last eight years, according to a report from the Institute of women's Policy Research (IWPR). Diversity in the workplace is essential. As stated above there are ten male entrepreneurs to every seven female entrepreneurs. In some countries, there are different rules about proper behavior for women in the workplace. The United States has come a long way regarding gender in the workplace. However, women are still not making the same income as men. There are more than 7.8 million Women-Owned Small Business (WOSB) in the United States. That's 29% of all America's business owners. Georgia, Maryland, Hawaii and the District of Columbia are the states with the largest percentage of women owned business.

Globalization in the Workplace

The United States attitude toward offshoring jobs is that it is a way of life that we have been accustomed to for many years. It supports global relationships with other countries and is a requirement for participating in that climate. Large business benefits from it because it maximizes cost, and it increases their profit margin. Some regular citizens have mixed feelings. Having a product produce at lower wages also reduce the cost the consumer may pay for that product but having that product made in another country takes job opportunities away from American citizens.

The United States has seen a decline in the industry jobs. Other countries that rely on those jobs for survival see off shoring as a good thing. Thanks to big businesses taking advantage of the low wages allows them to have work that they would otherwise not have. Offshoring can improve a developing country's way of life.

Government involvement in international business trade deeply affects a company's business activities. The different facets and layers of bureaucracy in trade regulation compliance can be overwhelming to many businesses. Oversight within the company ensures that the final product leaves the production facility and is exported legally.

The United States imposes trade sanctions on many countries involved in the international trade economy. "The Office of Foreign Assets Control (OFAC) of the US Department of the Treasury administers and enforces economic and trade sanctions based on US foreign policy and national security goals against targeted foreign countries and regimes, terrorists, international narcotics traffickers, those engaged in activities related to the proliferation of weapons of mass destruction, and other threats to the national security, foreign policy or economy of the United States" (U.S. Department of the Treasury, 2013). Many of these sanctions exist to protect the United States from exporting potentially threatening items and products to countries deemed to be dangerous to the United States or its allies.

The Export Administration Regulations enforced by the United States details trade regulations and restrictions to foreign countries and describes restrictions and regulations with re-exporting products originating from the United States to another country (Keller, 2012). One of these countries included on the list of hostile countries for U.S. trade sanction laws was Cuba until recently lifted by current US president.

The United States imposed their trade embargo against Cuba in 1960. This embargo was then passed into law in 1992 called the Cuban Democracy Act making trade with Cuba illegal as long as the Cuban government refuses to move towards democracy. The United States government also passed the Helms-Burton Act in 1996 restricting U.S. citizens from doing business with or in Cuba and preventing any type of assistance to the Cuban government. Trade restrictions include products such as nuclear equipment and material, chemicals, electronics and computer products, security products, lasers, navigation equipment, marine products, and space related items (Keller, 2012)., 2013).

Even though over the years trade restrictions and embargos have been decreased with Cuba, allowing more agricultural trade and American citizen interaction with family members in Cuba; tension and many trade restrictions still exist due to the opposing governmental and societal views between the United States and Cuba.

Understanding business trade encompasses the understanding that the reasons for a country intervening in free trade is not just for political reasons, but for cultural, economic, and safety reasons. The laws are there for the protection of trade not to impede on free trade. Until recently, President Obama lifted the sanctions against Cuba in 2015.

Another threat to small business is the Media and special interest groups-

Is the media really ethical and socially responsible? The media do have a code of ethics, but it is flexible.

The media is always hiding behind freedom of the press, freedom of speech and right to protect sources. They do not feel ethically obligated to the public except to give them information that they feel the public has a "right to know". As long as they are reporting their findings, they do not take into account the people that are being hurt or affected. It is important to ensure that you are reporting what is true and accurate. They exercise very little restraints and will go to any lengths for a story. The media should be sensitive to personal information of others and should keep certain things private. One would think that they would know how irresponsible and morally reprehensible they can be.

Media and special interest groups

Special interest groups can help as well as hurt our country. It all depends on their agenda. There was a time when special interest groups purpose were to bring attention to specific issues that otherwise would simply be ignored. Today, though, with the 24hr news cycle, the internet, and cell phones, some feel that they are not necessary. There are some good unbiased special interest groups that provide information to average citizens as well as political officials. They act as a liaison for a small group of individuals and take their ideas to public officials. However, there are some that are biased that outnumbered and out-funded by corporate-centric interest groups. Some of them have too much power and the politicians feel compelled to give them what they want and ignore what the general public wants. A few power people get what they want and leave the average American feeling as if the government is giving an unfair and disproportionate advantage to a chosen few.

Most are upset with Congress and political figures because they feel as if the government is less responsive to their needs. They feel that government favors the large businesses and organizations and affluent leaders. But the government favors small businesses too. There have recently been more funding to allow banks to lend to small businesses.

Special interest groups are going from being private power to public power. Money is raised during campaigns contributions, and the person who raises the most money has the most power. It has nothing to do with the average citizen's opinion. Special interest groups also lobby to get their problems and concerns heard by officials. Their sources of funds determine how far they get with the politicians. The National Small Business Association (NSBA is a nonpartisan advocacy group comprised of 65,000 members that advocate on behalf of entrepreneurs.

Getting started owning your business

There are several steps involved in starting and owning your own business. The steps all depends on what type of business you want to start and how large the business will be. One of the first things you should do is develop a mission statement and identify your brand. A mission statement defines who the customer is, what the organization purpose and function is, and what products or services they provide. It summarized what the organization wants to accomplish. A mission statement uses attractive, motivating words and is strong enough to catch a consumer's attention. One purpose is to drive customers to the business.

Brand differentiation is what sets a company brand apart from other companies that have a similar product. Brand differentiation helps identify a company's brand and position in the market. Most companies rely on price and service as their brand differentiation strategy. Anyone can sell something for less than the other company, and all companies claims they have good customer service. It does not matter how much something cost. The world is moving so fast, and this generation does not care about customer service. The price of a good is of no consequences when the product is well sought after. Consumers often ignore claims of good customer service and offerings of deals and low prices. They are immune to these strategies because they are empty promises, and every company makes them. "The value of a brand is not determined simply by sales; it is also determined by profitability."

Some experts believe that as little as 1% decrease in price actually is more detrimental to a company than raising that price by 1% (McDonald). Other experts believe that price strategy is good for short-term sales success but does nothing for building customer loyalty and repeat customers. For Example, a well–known shoe company can sell a pair of shoes for greater than $200 and young children of a lower socioeconomic class seems to figure out a way to get those shoes, proving that price is not a high indication for product brand protection. A coffee company can offer coffees at premium prices that people are willing to pay because the brand appealed to people's emotions.

A true brand differentiation strategist must understand what is needed to stand out from the competition in areas that matter most and that ensures that their brand has a lifelong survival. Find a strategy that gives a competitive edge that continues to drive service. A great deal of market research is needed to find the right brand differentiator.

Outdated strategic planning is inadequate for addressing today's turbulent times where markets move quickly, and competition is progressively ambiguous. Differentiation involves more than your fancy website, eye-catching logo, or slogan. Most companies do not need an elaborate ice cream truck or exciting billboards or even a Twitter page to flatter customers.

A signature difference or area of specialization can make your particular brand stands out from all the rest. The history of a brand keeps customers coming back time and time again. The competitors can consider trying to sell an idea and way of life, and not just a product. They can offer a similar service but in a distinct way, by not being afraid to combine the past, the present, and the future. They could try to appeal to different demographics or credit histories.

A smart business understands that the relationship that they have with the society in which they operate is directly responsible for their long term success. Customers not only expect good service at reasonable costs, but expect a business accountability to reflect socially. Investors similarly are looking for better economic growth that echoes their social and community relations.

Pricing is the first thing that a marketer have to consider. One reason is that the cost is involved from the beginning of forming the idea for a product or service to manufacturing the product to delivering the finished product for sale to the consumer. To guess wrong or to set the wrong price can contribute to the organizations' success or demise ultimately determining its survival. "Pricing is one of the most important elements of the marketing mix, as it is the only mix, which generates a turnover for the organization monetarily speaking."

Pricing affects all of the other P's such as product, place, and promotion. It takes money to develop and produce a product, to promote the product, and to determine the market to place for the product. Companies uses a pricing strategy to understand the highest price premium that they could sell their product for and to establish the price points that will maximize their revenue and profits. They must decide to use a national-account strategy to regulate pricing and make their pricing competitive. Concept Testing can be used to determine the prices as well.

If a similar product to your product can be found for $96-99 and your product is priced at $100, the other product will probably get chosen considering the only difference is the price of the two products. Chose to charge prices like $99 instead of $100 as a psychological effect to make the customer think that they are still getting that product for less than $100. Some companies decline when they have the option to set their prices higher than that of their competitors. Chose to use product line pricing to price different products at a different price point. Price products mid-line, understanding that a small decrease in the price will afford you a competitive edge and is imperceptible and does not affect profit margin.

Sometimes as a small business owner you have to compete with the other brand's popularity. Sometimes the competing brand has a long standing reputation, so even if the price is higher people sometimes goes with familiarity. A marketer has to consider the quality of their product. One can charge anything he wants but if the product is not appealing, the price is not the only thing that will sell it. The price has to be reasonable but practical.

Price Demand Mapping the Value

Usual market research generates important insight on the reaction to pricing strategy, and practical market information, resulting from price manipulations when using in-market price testing the value of the product or service. According to the U.S. Bureau of Labor Statistics Consumer Expenditure Survey, the average American family of four owns four cells phones, two computers, one iPad, two televisions, a listening device, and multiple video gaming consoles. Therefore the experts already know the price tolerance of the average consumers, and what consumers are willing to pay for a device of that sort. Marketers recognize the love for technology gadgets because of consumer's response to similar products eliminating the need for price discrimination. Please gather data from competitor response patterns to evaluate current price dynamics in the market when considering your product price.

Left only now with the challenge to determine how to make customers buy your products instead of the competitors' product by optimizing your brand, and making customers think your idea is worth more than the competitors'. Choose to price your products just right for the market. You should not use price skimming to price your product at the top of the market if it lacks exclusivity, and originality especially if you were not the first company to introduce that particular product.

A perceived value would have to be followed by quality and customer satisfaction. You must understand that you can price yourself right out of the market if your prices are too high. It would turn off buyers, or if you use penetration pricing, pricing your products too low, buyers will become suspicious that there is something wrong with the product or that it is not of high quality. You then need to make the decision neither to price too high, too low, nor to price the same. Decide to price somewhere in the middle. No one wants a cheap watered down version of another brand. You will need to know that you need to produce a product with the same quality, functionality, and styles as the existing products on the market but understand that your product have to be distinguished enough to warrant buyers to leave brands such as preexisting ones.

Business marketing

Marketing reflects the desires and wants of the consumer. A customer's decision to purchase is based on need to purchase, then want to purchase when buying goods and service. There are five stages a consumer moves through; need, recognition, information search, alternative to purchasing, post purchase behavior. A marketer has to know when to recognize where the consumer is and at what stage. As a marketer, you should evaluate what a customer is interested in the most or is purchasing the most. A good marketer is perceptive and thinks like a customer and are perceptive in noticing a customer's behavior. The more number of people want something the more people will want it. Consumers take advice from neighbors, friends, and advertisement in influencing their purchasing decision.

Marketing analysis is used to forecast sales. Correct sales forecasts smooth the progress of allocation of capital that is of short supply, making it more useful and efficient. The multiple regression technique is used as a statistical analysis that predicts the variability among two or more related variables when there are more than two factors which affects the behavior of a certain factor. Multiple regression methods allow for multiple predictor variables.

Correlation does not mean causation. Causation is the capacity of one variable to influence another, cause and effect. Correlation indicates the extent to which two variables tend to increase or decrease in parallel or move together. Correlation can be observed and therefore judged, but causation can be speculated but not necessarily proven simply because of correlating.

Correlation can be enough for someone to reach a conclusion and decision based on what is reasonable. An example of that could be that I tell my parents that there is a correlation between people with a larger than 40-inch waist and heart disease. This information may be enough for me to advise my parents to lose weight but it is not enough for me to definitively say that everyone who has a large belly will die from heart disease or to say that everyone who dies from heart disease has a big belly.

It is the same in the business world. Another example of correlation not being causation could be that the homeless population in one city may correlate with the crime rate but does not necessarily mean that that being homeless causes crime or being a criminal cause's homelessness.

There may be a third variable influencing the outcome such as the age of the population, unemployment rates, educational levels and morals. Understanding dependent and independent demand are very crucial to a company in ordering supplies and maintaining inventory. Dependent demand is the most common type of demand.

Calculations, such as MRP is needed to know its value. It means that demand for the product in question is influenced by the demand for some other product. An independent demand is something that will always exist even if there is no supply; one example is the demand for water. There has to be some knowledge of past demands. An independent demand is based on the history of the demands and confirmed demands by consumers.

Some companies have adopted programs and solutions that can auto-detect dependencies based on the independent demand for a product instead of using a manual method that is time-consuming. An independent demand can cause a dependent demand. An example of this is an end product, spare-parts such as an automobile.

Providing service to the customer

I believe that organization, business, and companies have an obligation to give the consumer as much information as possible. However, it is sometimes in the best interest of the customer that they do not have too much information, just enough relevant information. Information can be withheld if it is best to prevent panic of a community or if the information will cause unnecessary fear or anxiety.

Laws and regulatory provisions mandate that certain information is passed to the consumer such as how much of a chemical is in a product and if they chemical has potential for harm. Some consumers do not want to know, and they resent having the information. They accuse the government of violating their privacy by trying to warm them of harmful foods and cigarettes smoking. Each citizen thinks that it is their personal matter if they choose to purchase or consume an unhealthy product.

Business Owner Responsibility to the business-and paying yourself

As a business owner, you may also function as the operating manager. You may choose to pay yourself a salary or just take what is left at the end of paying the bills and taxes. As a manager, you may choose to use failure to meet your quota as an incentive to work harder for the next year. Even though this is highly practiced and acceptable business behavior, being able to double count inventory to reach your goal is taking the easy way out.

As a manager, you may want to receive a bonus every year. Sometimes people have the mindset that they are entitled to more than they actually deserve. As a manager, you will probably work hard but may need to work harder to stay within the budget to ensure you gets a bonus the following year.

I did things to increase my profitability such increase advertisement of merchandise, encouraged returning customers, or change the demographics of my targeted group. I thought about the option of increase the prices of the merchandise to increase the gross profits because that is always an option maybe not always the best option.

As a business owner, you should make sure that you are getting the merchandise at the best price. Instead of raising the prices, you can just buy it cheaper. Or you can buy it cheaper and still raise prices creating an even larger gross profit margin. Which I said is always an option, not always the best option. I suggest only doing this if it is your last resort. For example, if your business is in trouble or you need money to keep paying your employees.

Finding your location

Finding a location for your business is a challenge as well, and it is very important. This should be on the top of your list of things to do. You need to consider your needs. You may just need a small office space or an entire suite, you may even need an entire building. The location needs to be attractive to the customer and in a nice area of town. The building needs to be easily accessible with plenty of parking. You need to check out if there is a major highway near, if there is traffic and how much traffic. Check to see about foot traffic, and if the area is prone to a lot of crime. There need to be adequate street lighting if your business is operating during night hours. In my case, I did not want a business that you entered from the street for security reason. So I looked at buildings that had a lobby, already had established security and housekeeping services.

Your business needs to be visible with clear signs and directions. It does not matter how wonderful of a product you have if your customers can not find you. If people think that it is cumbersome or difficult to get through the door of your business, they will not come. People like convenience.

When looking for a location you may want to consider a high business area with other well-established businesses already present. One reason is that the area will already have people flow, already be business friendly, and the customers will see your business sparking their curiosity to what you have to offer. You can save money on advertisement and trying to attract customer to your business location because your presence will be an automatic advertisement.

You may want to put your business next to similar business but just make sure they are not your competition. This will help with zoning as well. If the similar business is there, it is likely that they have already paid for zoning inspections and the area is already zoned for your type of service. Which would save you a lot of work, time and money.

For example, my service is in health care so I can place my business next to other health and human service business for quick and easy referral. For example, if you are opening up a laboratory, it may be a good idea to have your business close to a physician office so if patients need to have lab work done, they can just do it without having to drive around. If you are opening up a pharmacy, the same concept applies.

Equally as important you may want to locate your business in a remote location if you are the only company that offers that service and customers will come to you because they have no other choice. The business location needs to fit the service that you are offering. The business you are opening and the style of the building has to fit. Choosing a college town may not be a good idea if you are selling medical assistive devices for the elderly. If you are opening up an adult entertainment shop, a complex next to a church, Christian bookstore, or elementary school may not be a good idea.

Do your homework, so you will know the demographics of the area too. You may want to consider having a person available on staff who can speak multiple languages. There are more than 47 million people in America with limited English proficiency. This number does not just include foreign-born Americans or immigrants but aging population. If you are opening up a food store, you may want to make sure you sell food that people in that neighborhood wants to buy and eat.

When looking for a location, price has to be considered. You may need to negotiate a lease so remember to budget for furniture, decorations, and unexpected expenses. Factor in all the cost and the size. Underestimating the cost and size could hurt in the long run if your business location cannot accommodate expansion or growth. With my personal experience having too much space is better than not having enough space eliminating the need to move later and reestablishing a customer base.

This is one thing that I considered when looking for a location for my business. I wanted to know how far it was going to be from my home. This may not be the best idea for you if you may want to move in the near future. So do not let that be the only reason you chose that location. Although it is mighty nice living within walking distance from where I work.

Once you have found a place and procured zoning you would want to make sure you have adequate licensures to do the type of business you want. Selling things like alcohol requires federal and state licensure. Each state has their own requirements. Some counties within the state has requirements as well. The requirements may vary from county to county so make sure you know your local laws. It would be a shame to start a business then find out that you cannot do it because that locale does not allow that type of business.

Do not forget to contact the Internal Revenue Service (IRS) for a tax ID number or EIN if you are planning to hire employees. The United States Small Business Administration (SBA.gov) website has information as well, and every state have local offices where you can get help obtaining the proper license for you locale.

There are also seminars and workshops that you can attend to get that information. These seminars will also offer help in deciding if you want to form a corporation or simply a DBA, "doing business as". One thing that a lot of prospective entrepreneurs do not include in their business plan is trademark or service mark their business name or logo. You need to copyright any advertisement flyers or commercials you make for your business. And patent all inventions. You may want to obtain accreditation if you plan to operate a business that will be accepting medical payments from Medicare & Medicaid Services.

Funding

Your

Dream

$$Please

Give$$

Funding your Business

Another challenge to doing a start-up business is finances. You need money to get started and that amount of money needed is dependent on the type of business you are starting. The most prudent way for me was to finance it myself. You can choose to ask family and friends, or obtain small loans which are hard to get from a bank without collateral. You may need to have good credit. A micro loan for small businesses is still possible just very difficult. You can also ask strangers to help you raise money by using crowdfunding like gofundme.com, and StartSomeGood.com

Some people take the risk and borrow from or withdraw money from their retirement account. This is not recommended by me unless you are positive that the business that you are starting up is going to be very successful. Remember this is your retirement so if your business fail you would have lost retirement money that you cannot get back.

Obtaining funding can be done by considering investors. I did it myself while still working my regular job. Experts advise against using or crossing over your personal money with business expenses, but I wanted to be able to launch without owing anyone anything and without a whole a lot of people knowing my plans. I kind of wanted my business to be a shock factor. So I paid for things out of my current income earned from working. Those things included my business and zoning license and permit, the first year's lease on my building, furniture, equipment, and supplies. I also loan myself money to my business that my business can pay me back once it started making money.

33% of small businesses rely heavily on credit for financing. Wholesaler financing may allow you to get goods and products on credit then pay them back as you sell the items, or you may be able to exchange goods for service such as bartering. Most people still finance their business using friends and family.

Finding investors-

An investor would be interested in the return on their investment. It would use the information gathered to make judgments about the company's ability to provide data on past investments and profits, and cash flow potential. An investor, unlike a creditor, may want to know if the company or enterprise is complying with governmental regulatory agencies. A creditor would want to know what the risk is when lending money to an enterprise. The financial accounting information is useful in determining a company's ability to repay the money.

Some business apply for small government grants. These will require you to do some research, and often times write long grant proposals and adhere to some restrictions.

Who to hire

Help Wanted

So now that you have perfected your business plan, you have found your location, and have all of the supplies you need, you are ready to open for business, but wait you need help in the office. Now it is time to hire your first employee. You can always ask dear old grandma to man the phones for you, and you can solicit your son or daughter to empty the trash, refill the copier, and vacuum the floors. But really? How do you go about deciding how many staff member to hire????

Know your state laws and hiring practices. Identify employment classification. There are questions you need to ask yourself concerning hiring employees. How many staff do you need? How many full time; how many part time? How many as needed staff? How many contractor staff? Some states have at at-will laws. That means an employer can terminate any employee at any time for any reason or for no reason. The employee has no right to challenge the termination. How does that affect me? However, federal law protects employees from discrimination because of age, race, sex, religion, national origin, or handicap.

Do you want to interview and hire perspective employees yourself or do you want to use an agency, or outsource to a human resources department.

Small business owners often have businesses in remote locations. Prospective employees may live outside of the immediate area, and it becomes difficult to travel for an interview. There are ways to be present without being physically present using computers to eliminate barriers of time and space. Having a computer-mediated interview is convenient because it saves money and time. It saves a lot of money in travel expenses. There may be things that you, as the manager, can invest in to get started. You may want to start by purchasing things such as a computer, phone lines, video equipment, internet services, and a cell phones with texting capabilities. All of these devices can be used to take advantage of modern advancements in technology such as distance meetings and learning webinars. Face to face is still best, the quickest, and more accurate. It provides instant feed- back. A video is best if used for an initial screening interview but should be followed by a traditional face to face interview.

If you decided to hire your own staff, you would be faced with making the organization appeal to the public. Find the right employee or let them find you. How can you attract new employees? You can always advertise offering bonuses, incentives, and money.

Money is not the strongest motivator however it is often used when it comes to trying to attract potential employees to your organization. Money is also a good motivator to convince them to stay especially if they have gained extra knowledge or education while employed there. However, money is not a good motivator and maybe even a cheap insult when trying to get people to do things your way. They may see it as you are trying to buy them, control their behavior and are waving money in front of them like a dog lover waves a bone. Money as a motivator can fix a short-term problem.

You may be faced with the decision to hire a seasoned, recently laid off person for more pay, or a new graduate, inexperienced, younger staff for less pay. You may have to consider and accommodate people with non-traditional life styles, and schedules.

With globalization, teleworking and the growth of the internet, advanced technology has made it easier for people to multitask and work from a distance. As a hiring manager, you may have to accept people with an education from a different type of school, or education platform that are offered, not brick and mortar as we were used to. It is possible that the school may even be overseas or abroad.

Learning a different language maybe a big issue as the economy has taken so many jobs abroad. Cultural diversity at its best using resources, retaining, requalification, recruiting, and restructuring----the right person. Flexibility teamwork communication is another good philosophy to possess.

You should be involved in the hiring process if possible. Using a hands-on approach to recruiting new staff that is very beneficial. You will get to meet the possible staff members before they even apply for the job. It is almost as if the staff is being hand-picked for your company. One of the things that was important to me was being able to view various college's curriculum and determine if the courses are in line with what a perspective employee should be learning.

As a recruiter for my own business I get to see if the person is a good fit and the person gets to see if they are attracted to my organization and supports my vision as well as the mission on my company. Having the time and opportunity to visit different college campus showed that I cared enough to get involve with the community as I attempt to sell my brand.

The Importance of Job Descriptions

Are job descriptions still needed? Why or why not? The purpose of job description policy will have a complete job description of assigned duties, required and preferred experiences and skills. Management reserves the right to add or assign additional duties as necessary that are not outside the scope of practice for the employee.

Job descriptions are still a tool needed to describe what the job specific functions entails and acts a plan to let the perspective employee know exactly what the organization is looking for. A detailed job description can be a tool for someone who is in school to know what they need to concentrate on in their studies to be suited for that job upon graduation. Jobs descriptions also serve legal functions. The American with Disabilities Act of 1982 allows for the request of special accommodations to fit certain job descriptions. Companies with well-written job descriptions can refer to those descriptions when evaluating employee's performance.

Should all training be acquired prior to hiring an employee? How much money does your company have to devote to training a new employee? What about the risk; do you know if you are willing to risk bringing someone aboard that lacks the necessary skills to perform the job? How do you make that determination? As a hiring manager you will have to choose between training options, carefully selecting the best value. How can one evaluate what training is needed and determine the best value?

Before determining what employees need to be trained or retrained, as a manager you have to assess to see what the training needs are for your organization. There may be a need for training for a new plan being implemented by that organization or some change in a law or requirement by a state or regulatory agency. You have to first determine what the set goals are for the training to decide what staff members will be affected by the training. You have to determine the cost of the training and what training materials are suitable for the training. Then evaluate the cost to see if the training of employees is worth the initial amount spent. Sometimes it is difficult to determine the return on investment where training is concerned. Assessment of the employees that need to be trained should include the employee's current position and whether the employee is planning to continue to work for you long-term.

Workplace Diversity

Workplace diversity creates an environment where various racial, ethnical, and groups can work together as they each contribute their different talents and perspectives. You may need to adjust your operating procedures to accommodate and embrace these differences. As a manager, you can facilitate and emphasize group goals where diversity increases creativity. You may see it necessary to adjust your hiring process to include more women, people of different age groups, and people of different ethnic backgrounds.

Understanding the challenges faced with being in a male dominate world, I strive to make sure that my organization is well diverse, by hiring an equal number of women and minorities. I make sure that staff are well trained by offering them the educational and training opportunity to improve.

Management styles

What kind of manager do you plan to be? Have you considered what management style best fits your personality or fit the type of business you manage?

Have you worked in an organization that segmented talent as a foundation for their investment in employee development? The workplace planning approach included segmented talent. It allowed for the skilled level or recognized talent of some employees to be balanced with the less experience staff. One instance that is often used is having a person in charge of the shift or acts as the lead. This person usually has more years' experience and shows leadership talent. The rest of the staff for that shift consists of some newly graduate care givers and others that skill levels are somewhere in the middle. There are benefits and drawbacks to this approach.

One of the positives of segmented talent is that it aids in the re-engineering of a department. It can be used when there is a need to move some employees into a higher position. One of the negative would be to consider inclusive versus exclusive. Some would say that it may cause the department to have a *"clique"* atmosphere. The use of the terms "talented" and "non-talented" are sometimes seen as offensive.

Once I have hired the right employee, I plan to keep them. Employee retention and longevity is very important to me. I wish to allow my employees to grow as my business grow.

A good motivator to encourage people to do a good job is to give them recognition and praise for a job well done. An employee will focus on improvements once they have established that they are satisfied, have pride with their job and have the respect of their peers. An opportunity for a promotion or status change may encourage a staff member to work harder and become more productive.

One good thing about being an employee in someone else company before becoming an entrepreneur is that I understand how things are from an employee's point of view and I treat people the way I want to be treated. I am more sympathetic to employees and their needs. Employees want to feel as though their opinions count. I want to be able to trust my employees.

Laissez-faire style of management would be best when staff has entrepreneur qualities and can follow directions. This style of management is when it is important to have a strong staff to trust that can basically run the office with little or no supervision.

If for some reason you, as manager, is not able to be present as much as you like, or fear that the staff cannot carry on in your absence, you can be present even if not physically. You can implement things to maintain visibility in all of your location.

Surveillance, or using something similar to what parents do when they want to spy on the nanny. You can install camera or video monitoring throughout the facility, keeping an eye on the staff. The manager can have two-way communication such as intercom, instant messaging, or push to talk cell phones to answer any questions needed by the staff and guide them step by step.

A good retention motivator is giving the employee a little autonomy to show that their actions are trusted without strict supervision. The emotional effect of an employee feeling trusted, respected, and liked, is far greater than the motivation of money. Paying for a temporary fix may become too costly for an organization in the end. Having to keep paying people to do what you want them to do is a problem that may arise.

Often employees chose a place to work for reasons other than money. Most of the time their employment choices are based on the job being matched with their skills. Money as a motivator is good if money is what is needed to survive and fulfill the basic living expenses. Money is very important, and it is necessary if you do not have any. A business should pay an employee what they are worth from the start of employment to avoid having to have the raise the threat of leaving or money discussion later.

Employee retention should encourage engagements. Some companies tends to state that they want to motivate their employees by encouraging them to become more engaged. However, when an effort is made to get more involved in the decision-making, the individual is made to feel isolated and rejected. I work for a company where there are several co-workers that are awful at their jobs, but they get all of the praise.

Employee engagements in business meeting are important to the organization. One strategy would be to encourage employees to each lead one of the meetings with a plan or idea that they want to implement. They can work as a team to come up with the idea, or they can do it as individuals. I would make the information sharing interesting and encourage communication and feedback amongst the staff. I would choose a time that is convenient for everyone. There are important tips to keep in mind.

o Make sure that there are clear rules for decision making using a group of diverse back grounds and varying experience and educational levels. Group think in this situation could be avoided by assigning one person to present the advantages or pros while another person presents the cons of the topic. Outside sources with greater knowledge should have been allowed to come in and present their finding.

o Organizations are always changing some without recognizing first-order change and second order change. Changing structures does not guarantee success if the current persons involved are not willing to modify their strategy or way of thinking, core values, and mission of the organization. Organizations have to determine if they want their changes to be based on anticipatory or reactive. Structural changes need to occur to keep up with the changes in technology, and the demands of the customers and the external environment. The strategy is a behavior that must be change before implementing a new structure. The attitude and readiness for change must be present for the new strategy to be effective.

o As a manager, discrimination of information responsibility to employees is important. Failure to discriminate leads to wasting time on useless information. It sends employees going into all different direction with no clear path to the intended goal. I have experience this all too often. I have had the pleasure or displeasure of working under mangers that were a very nice people but very poor leaders. One manager would chuck and jive, spends lots of time talking but saying nothing. He and a chosen few would know what was going on, but the rest of us would be left in the cold. You would come to work one day, and things would have change. When you ask "when did we start doing that?" someone would yell out "we been start doing that where have you been?"

While presented with the responsibility and task of developing an organizational change, the first step was to assess the company and analyze the current systems in place to determine what areas the changes are needed mostly. The kind of assessment tools used are public reputation, past experiences, complaints, observations, employees and communication effectiveness.

According to the Salovey, Mayer and Caruso four-branch model of emotional intelligence, establishing solid interpersonal relationships permit leaders to drive motivation and inspire confidence and enthusiasm with his employees. Correctly evaluating and articulating emotions makes sure the communication is effective between persons and offers them with a greater understanding of the people they work with. Building an environment of collaboration and teamwork improves sensitivity to emotions allows employees to be extra supportive of the manager's decisions and the organization's objectives.

An organizational design is defined as the entails of the "formal and the informal structures and processes within an organization". An organizational design is an outline from which an organization functions. The character of the organization design is influenced by internal and external forces. An organizational design displays an organization's size, structure, and processes. There will be no need to incur millions of dollar cost for the new system, and that is not justified when the enforcement of the current system can be easily applied.

Communication with employees

Organizational silence

I would not say that I am guilty of "groupthink" but there were times when I want to speak out and I look around to observe the body language of my co-workers or even the mood of my manager before saying what I thought. Everyone wants to get along with everyone else and everyone wants to be politically correct. So we tend to go along with whatever the majority wants. One fear that I have noticed in my workplace was when we had an intimidating manager or if there was pressure from management to make the best decision.

We assume that everyone is in agreement since no one speaks out. This is call the illusion of unanimity. I have felt this before. I wanted to say something but did not want the others to think that I am being difficult and hard to please. Peer pressure reminds me of a television show where the jury's votes is 11 to 1 and the one person that is holding out is pressured by his peers to change his mind. We had this thing that we used to at work called "best friends" at work. I thought this was a bad idea because you felt like your personal friendship was threatened if you spoke out about a work issue that did not agree with your friend's view.

Managers can facilitate ways to communicate effectively with their employees all the while encouraging their employees to communicate face-to-face, written, or whichever method is most comfortable. A manger wants to communicate with her staff, whether it is verbal or written. It is important for the manager to possess good writing skills. When a manger communicates with her staff she wants to be understood. She should use active voice but make sure that she uses language that is understood by all. She should refrain from using slang words or jargon because different cultures uses different meaning with slang words. Proper grammar would be nice because the staff would like to know that their manger is smart enough to be their leader. Using active voice will allow a manager to be direct and to the point.

o A persuasive message delivered face-to- face has the advantage of the observance of body language that help convey the message and tone of voice. An email can be effective when it comes to referencing the e-mail for missed or forgotten information. Non- written communication may be difficult to remember. Having a written email can be helpful in reviewing for future questions. The email can serve as a "contract" so to speak; binding the sender to the exact words that he or she cannot deny once it is written, and it allows for mass distribution of information that has to be said only once. A persuasive email can be as effective as a face-to-face message as long as it is not an emotional message.

o A persuasive email can be effective if the sender conveys the message expectations for positive outcomes and convince the reader that he or she stands to benefit from the message. Personalize the message by using the voice of the "you" attitude will make the reader think that you are concerned about their involvement. Be sure you know your audience. Keep the email professional but not boring.

o A sender of a persuasive email should use the direct request pattern stating the purpose of the email. Identify the problem including some solutions. Ask for the action you want but make sure you do not make the reader feel like he or she is being dictated to. Maybe it would be helpful to mention some of the past successes to remind the staff but do not make the email too long.

o A persuasive message delivered face-to-face has the advantage of the observance of body language that help convey the message and tone of voice. An email can be effective when it comes to referencing the e-mail for missed or forgotten information. Non- written communication may be difficult to remember.

There is more evidence that email communication has more advantages. The staff will see their manager as confident and honest and the reader can visualize what the manager wants them to do. The manager should put statements in positive form so the message can be received positively. It is easier to motivate the staff using constructive criticism that is more productive than just criticizing what has not been achieved or done. Positive language can make the worse news or message seem better. Effective writing will ensure more cooperation and collaboration from the staff.

Positive language by the manager tells the staff what can be done instead of reminding them what has not been done. Positive language sounds more helpful than judgmental. I have had the displeasure of working with managers that are brutal and complained a lot. It did not make the staff want to improve and it did not increase morale. She constantly used phrases that implied that we were stupid like; "I don't understand how you guys can't get it right or "I fail to understand why you can't do it", it's not rocket science."

A manager should use honesty and encourage communication even if the situation is a bad one. People who trust their manager can tell if he or she is having problems understanding the task that was given. Open communication gets the job done better than everyone feeling ashamed and embarrassed. A manager should be approachable by using positive language.

Direct and indirect inquiry can balance each other causing a shift from automatic thinking to active thinking. Use direct method for e-mails to clarify difficult to understand information. The direct method is used in differentiating between ambiguity as ignorance and ambiguity as confusion. The tone is professional and short to the point. A direct method is good for getting things done that are of an urgent matter. Audiences that are expecting good news prefer the direct method. The inquiry is usually upfront and the speaker or writer sound very confident and sure of the statements being made.

The tone of the indirect inquiry is more passive and is used when delivering bad news. This approach is also used when the writer does not want to appear arrogant. The style of this writing is to lead into the subject with facts and findings before presenting your conclusion and proposal.

How to motivate employees-

If you have an employee that is not motivated and does not care about his work; or he has been underperforming and has shown lack of attention to office policies and procedures, make sure that you have made the expectations clear and that he is not getting mixed signals. He needs made aware of your expectation, hence avoiding him seeking attention by means of doing a task to please despite not knowing all of company policies and procedures. If lack of motivation and unclear directions are not present, then maybe the employee will have a better performance as well as a better attitude while working. The morale would go up, and everything would improve tremendously.

Another reason for a disengaged employee could be a lack in the management structure or if some of the employee's needs are not being met. The employee belongingness needs, esteem needs, and self-actualization needs will not be met if the employee feels inferior. If he feels that his managers do not know him well enough because they are focused on getting promoted as well as him.

In this case the employee needs to have someone that treats him like an individual and not just an employee which will help him to feel at ease; instead of feeling like everything is based on performance and perfection - but have some level of personality to it in such a way that unity arises and positive attitudes grow.

As a manager you may ask yourself what changes might improve the employee's motivation? The changes needed are to have the company not base everything on performance, but to focus on the person. These can be done in a number of ways: Firstly, improvement in company's structure. There are several other approaches a company can take to correct an employee's behavior. The first would be to allow the employee to self-correct.

The manger should refresh each employee of their expectations and job description responsibilities. Encourage adequate feedback and allow questions and comments. After a specific time period has pasted, the manager can reevaluate the behavior and then evaluate for need for additional job training. Otherwise implement the progressive disciplinary policy leading to termination if the quality of work does not improve.

Management structure

When comparing the management structure of one company to that of the management dynamics of another company, it may be clear to see how having a different management structure yields different results. Effective management is essential but is not the only excuse for one's poor performance. An employee's behavior displays whether he does or does not care to do a better job. If his behavior is reckless in regard to company policies, then he is probably headed for disciplinary action. The manager needs to engaged in effective communication and ask for clarification in his duties and expectations. The employee owes it to himself to become more involved and responsible for his own success. He can "read" the company's policies if he is not familiar with them.

Communication in this aspect is important. The manager may need to show more empathy and respect for the job that is the employee is actually doing. It would be nice if the manager motivates and empowered each employee to succeed. However, only the employee can increase his motivation at this point. He has to want to do the best job he can. This may mean making an extra effort or it may mean approaching his managers with the concerns that his needs as an employee are not being met. He needs to communicate his lack of feeling like part of the team and the gap between leader and worker needs to be bridged. Compare his needs or review Maslow's Hierarchy of needs to fully identify where he belongs. He can also ask to attend some training seminars alone or accompanied by his managers.

Training and seminars are a good way to learn how to effectively be a good leader and also how to be a better employee. Attending training seminars would help learn communication skills needed to effectively communicate with his superiors and subordinates. Attending seminars and training will help the managers better communicate with employees and learn other skills that will help them become better managers to current and other future employees. The company, can learn from other companies by reading their success stories or undergoing similar training. They can learn that profits are important but the relationship and reputation a company has with the community and its staff should parallel their business success.

A forced distribution model can be effective as analysis or if the goal is to incorporate a more rigorously discipline model to the organization's performance ratings or implement a succession plan. It can be used to motivate employees, but the supervisors of the organization used their judgment in determining where the employee is grouped using terms like the "top 20% " or the "bottom half".

Determining a person's ranking or placing a person is a certain tier may actually force them to do better in order to move to the next tier or it may not. It may cause low morale if peers are pitted against each other. A straight expectation appraisal approach that identifies gaps in performance may be a better choice than forced distribution.

What to offer your employees-Employee benefits package

What benefits do you want to give employees? A manager can offer employee assistance with health, wellness, family concerns such as counseling, and Healthcare is one of the most important assistance an organization can offer. The return for healthy employees benefits the employee as well as the company. What options does companies have for lowering their costs in providing employee health care coverage?

It is amazing to me how organizations are responding to the Affordable Care Act of 2010. The companies that does not want to cover their employees will reduce the employee's hours to keep them from being eligible for benefits. They also reduce their contributions by hiring part-time or as needed seasonal workers. Companies can offer lower health care premiums for employees that do not smoke. They have incentives for employees that participate in wellness programs. Companies can allow employees to buy their insurance through a private health insurance exchange.

There are personal things an individual can do to lower premiums. Sometimes it is hard to do when you have a group policy but and individual policy may work. I always tailor my insurance according to my needs. I do not plan to have any more children so I will get a policy that does not include maternity. I think that if a company can afford to and most of them can, they should provide health insurance to their employees. If not, they should at least connect them to resources that can assist them in finding an individual policy that fit their needs.

How can management improve work environment?

Will your newly hired employees work from home or come to the office? It is important that your place of work is safe. This safety is related to the environment of an organization that a person has to work in. There are several dynamics that affects the well-being and safety of employees. These include but not limited to "personal safety equipment, installation of equipment controls, creation and dissemination of operational manuals, policies of hazardous materials handling, adoption of drug and alcohol testing policies, introduction of employee counseling services, and implementation of safety training programs are all utilized by companies to minimize their incidences". Managers are sent to training and education classes and the title for this person is "safety manager."

There are other things that a manager can do to improve the work environment for the employees like reducing stress. Three out of every four American workers define their work as stressful. In fact, job-related stress has remained defined as a "global epidemic" by the United Nations' International Labor Organization.

Stress is defined as contact among personalities within their environment. Engagements at work should be a positively stimulating encounter for most people, but it can similarly be negative. Work can be an incredible place filled with stressors. Stress at work can effect productivity. It can cause one to have low morale and not want to come to work. The stress can also escalate into something stronger such as violence. The work place can cause many individuals harm emotionally and physically.

More than 2 million American fall victim of workplace violence every single year. Office violence can happen anyplace, and no one is exempt. Some employees remain at greater risk. These are workers who handle money in public such as street vendors, transport commuters such as taxi drivers or bus drivers.

Do I need a lawyer?

Most tasks that need to be done by a person starting their own business can be done without a lawyer. Things like choosing and registering a business name, searching and researching databases for trademark information, establishing a DBA "doing business as", applying for business licenses and zoning, forming an LLC, applying for a domain name or website, interview and hiring employees and fill out IRS paperwork.

Hiring a lawyer may not be necessary to start and open your business but it is well advised. It is a good idea to have an attorney on retainer for complicated questions and concerns that may arise. Having a lawyer on standby as a precaution is a good idea. A lawyer can help you draft papers and help you understand hiring laws. A lawyer can help you with contracts if you have a business partner. It is good to have one available if you are getting sued or being investigated by The U.S. Securities and Exchange Commission (SEC).

Reporting The

$$$$$$$$$$$$$$$$$$$$$$$$$$$$

Business assets business earnings and reporting statements.

The U.S. Securities and Exchange Commission (SEC) has standards for businesses. Assets reporting is one of those standards. The most significant assets are those of liquidity value. These are assets that can quickly be turned into cash. This may include equipment that can be sold, interests on short term investments, and receivable income. Larger companies may view their employees and their reputation as very significant assets.

The most significant non-current asset of a business is any trademarks or patents they may own. They may also have long-term investment in real estate property, investment in other companies.

o Is there an advantages of having large cash balance? Short answer is, yes. When growth is slow and profits are down, companies may need to dip into their reserve fund. These expenses may include payroll, payment to their lenders and payment to cover other expenses. In this case, it is necessary and advantageous to have some large cash on hand and not have to borrow it.

o Are there any disadvantages of having large cash balance? The short answer is, yes. When companies hoard money, they are neither lending nor borrowing. When cash is said to be "parked", it translates to a slow economy or it stagnates economic growth. Banks and large business claim economic hardship even though they can sometimes have trillions of dollars in reserve that they refuse to reinvest to give our economy the boost it may need. Monies that is available as immediate cash may not be eligible to earn interest at the same rate as an investment.

o What companies currently have sizable amounts of cash and liquid investments on their balance sheets? Banks are one of the businesses that have large cash on hand. A bank may be slow to lend because they do not feel confident in the economy and are afraid to make investments. These companies all have large cash balances on hand according to Chief Executive.Net Oil companies such as ExxonMobil $52 billion, Chevron $43 billion, and ConocoPhillips $ 45 billion, Google $44 billion and Apple $ 117 billion (2012).

The standard definition of financial management is "the efficient and effective management of money or funds in such a manner as to accomplish the objectives of the organization and being concerned with, and able to manage a company's asset, liabilities profitability, and cash flow."

Strategic financial management entails taking measures that include the knowledge of an organization's assets. Making financial decisions by identifying the company's resources, analyzing data, and having clear objectives. It is important to identify any variance in budgeted results by monitoring and comparing actual results with the budgeted results. Personal management of funds are similar to that of business.

Cash flow can determine if an individual feels financially secure and if they can predict and prevent personal financial downfalls. Having free cash flows helps an individual choose what to purchase, from whom to purchase, and how much to pay for that purchase. Personal finances are a little more difficult when dealing with investments and the stock market. Before you can understand and successfully manage a business finance you may want to be able to handle your own finances.

Personal business accounting

Personal knowledge is understanding how the market works. The financial crisis that the country is currently in is slower than the usual cycle. Normally every economy has peak and troughs. When the economy is sluggish it is usually normal to keep investing because you know that the economy will recover soon. In the recent wake of the current financial state of the country, people are reluctant to invest or spend money. It is understandable to be driven by fear when it comes to money. We should do the total opposite according to most financial experts. We should continue to pump money into the economy, sort of like the old "priming the pump" rationale.

Having a job is almost golden and the fear of not being able to find another one or finding another one just to have the company go out of business is causing hesitation when contemplating changing careers. However, four years is about a safe vesting period in the business world. Most people who have been on their job for more than four years, are not going to leave for fear. There are several web sources that are interesting and explains some of the reason people's past experiences with money is controlling their current investing decisions. Just remember to keep good accounting records especially if you want to use investors.

The Financial accounting information is used by both the investor and creditor. Some of the information is useful to both groups in order to make decisions about the enterprise, judge the value, quality or worth. Both groups find it necessary to learn about the monetary assets of the industry they are interested in. Both groups look at how the company fulfills their obligations, along with behavior of the company in how they pay their bills, treat others and maintain their responsibility to the public. Both groups need to find out what an enterprise is intended for. Although, both the investor and creditor have similar requirements for use of some information, they each also need distinctive information that is prevalent to their function.

Accounting standards are necessary to ensure the quality financial reporting. The primary function of accounting is to maintain data and communicate economic information about a business or enterprise. This information is used by investors, shareholders, merchant, creditors, the consumer and the community.

This financial information is used by investor and creditor to take decisions. It is important for this information to be accurate and of high standards for the investors and stakeholders make informed, efficient decisions that are in their best interest. There are several methods used.

The indirect method is also referred to as the reconciliation method. The steps include initially taking the net income and then converting to the net cash flow all from operating activities that affect the reported net income but not the affected cash.

Overstating bad debt will result in the overestimating allowance for bad debt, overstating operating expenses, understating net income, and understating account receivables. The manager should not overestimate his bad debt because it will decrease his net income even if he feels he needs to do it to qualify for a loan

An attempt to defraud by intentionally omitting the facts is unethical behavior. Any intentional fraud is against the law and can result in penalties, fines and jail time. Overstating gross profits, overstating ending inventory, overstating total assets, and understating cost of goods sold are all results of double counting on balance sheets. Any intentional misrepresentation of the facts is unethical. Business have to behave ethically.

A Code of Ethics policy is a standard of behavior that is implemented as a guide used by businesses, professional associates, prospective stakeholders, and the establishment's administrative officers and personnel. An effort to encourage better proficiency and productivity, between workers and potential consumers, an organization's Code of Ethics should serves as a road map to guide associates to be aware of their individual action and behavior. And how these behaviors affect the encounter with potential customers or clients.

Some possible consequences of Double counting inventory can result in the manager being accused of fraud. Fraudulent behavior is punishable by law, meaning that the manager can go to jail. The company may get a bad reputation and experience loss of business, licensures, and certifications and sanctioned by state or federal regulatory agencies. There are ways to detect discrepancies in reporting.

The manager's reports can be reviewed and compared to the previous years' report to detect double counting inventory. Discrepancies and red flags will go up if there seem to be a very large dollar amount of profits and a decrease in the cost of goods sold. Any inconsistencies may be cause for concern.

There are benefits to overstating debt and understating income, however. A company can use the artificial income used as understated income in one reporting period if they intend to overstate that same income in another period. It is just like juggling money around, not cooking the books. It is very important that you know what you are doing to minimize mistakes.

Companies are allowed to use income smoothing to make it look like they have consistencies in their profits. This behavior is acceptable. Would an investor ever know if a company is understating or overstating income or debt? I guess it is understood and investors already know that companies indulge in this practice and they are probably doing it themselves.

High-quality and valuable financial reporting information must encompass the necessary distinctiveness, and easy to understand. The information must be comparable to similar information. A good indication that a business is in good financial health is how much assets it has and its ability to convert that assets into cash. Another good indicator would be the buisness' ability to pay their short-term debts. Short term debts can be things such as supplies, employee wages and interests.

A company needs to be able to show that the cash flow coming in is equal to or less than the cash flow going out just as you would with your own personal budget. If you need two thousand dollars per month going to rent, utilities, automobile insurance groceries, and car note, then you need to have at least two thousand dollars' worth of cash flow coming in the household to meet those obligations. It is better for a business and an individual to show extra or disposable, residual income for cases of unexpected costs or emergencies. A lender looks at a potential borrower ability to pay their bills on time. Some of the things that may be red flags to a lender would the lack of disposable income, the inability to pay on time in the past, the lack of emergency funds equal to or greater than the amount owed each month, the length of time or documented cash flow, and the amount and consistency of the cash flow.

My experiences have been overwhelming to say the least. My small business is health care related and billing, collecting and reporting finances is very challenging. So please elicit help like I did. You can hire an accountant and business lawyer. It was very helpful understanding health care economics. When collecting and reporting money, it is important to maintain confidentiality and security too. It was important to me to secure my financing information as well as the health information of my clients.

Information Technology

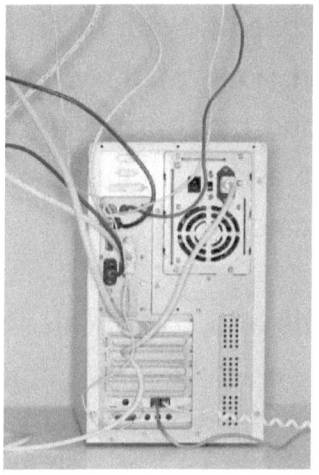

Information technology is not a new concept although its use is now spreading rapidly. It is the creation and designing, development, implementation and managing and support of computer- based information. This information can be helpful in maintaining and running an organization.

Information technology applications are used in business to help them get organized. Information technology is the development, installation, and implementation of computer systems and applications (Wikipedia). When people think of implementing an information technology system, they immediately think of some sophisticated elaborate computer program that is very costly. But there are simple areas of business that need the aid of an information technology application. One of those areas of need may be maintaining and monitoring employee work hours. Staffing needs and availability is one such area that needs organizing.

Working out the details of a complicated schedule is the first part of a schedule situation, but communicating those details to others can be a challenge of its own. Choosing the correct application to implement a schedule is very important.

At what point should you decide if your organization is in need of an information technology application to help you manage staffing? You should consider some facts concerning the type of organization you are in, the number of employees involved, and whether or not those employees work rotating or stationary shifts. If you manage a group that works on projects with milestones or events, such as meetings, sub-task, or even your employees' time, you've probably struggles with putting together complicated scheduling information and communicating the arrangements to others. Arrange or organize the job assignments for a whole week. You can use a simple downloadable template to shade and combine cells to easily distinguish shifts, or utilize assignment codes to prepare a revolving agenda for each work day.

The initializing of an information technological systems application will require some cost. This cost varies depending on need and the size of your facility. This cost can include hardware and software purchases. There are templates that can be downloaded directly from the internet free of charge. Download, at no cost, employee work schedule spreadsheets to help systematize job assignment. Those such templates were intended for small businesses and are predominantly functional for restaurants that serve fast food, small retail stores, or departments where the staff rotates stations during a work day.

Other programs come with a fee of some sort. This can be a very small nominal fee, or it can be a little more expensive, depending on your need and availability of funds. There are also cost that is associated with the training of personnel that will be using the system. This too will also vary with the number of staff that is involved. There are hundreds of templates in multiple shifts format.

When implementing any change within your organization, it is important to consider the barriers. You will be faced with personnel that may not want to change and is comfortable with the system the way that it is. You will need to carefully present the idea to them with supporting evidence of its important and functionality. Some barriers and obstacles associated with the implication of a scheduling system can be cost if funds for your organization are limited. There will be time to set aside to train other personnel on using the new system. Whether you need to put together on a small meeting or complex schedule of employee shifts, you can use the tools included to help you concentrate on your scheduling task

Consider the need for adjustments and changes when deciding on the appropriate information technology application to choose. Are there staff members that will soon be removed from the list? Is there a possibility of someone resigning soon or the hiring of new employees? If you anticipate the need to make changes, you should choose an application that is easy to manipulate. Some templates are highly customizable. You can add several amounts of rows to the spreadsheet depending on how many employees you have. You can insert columns to generate a 24-hour schedule. Tailor the key with your own list of task. You can communicate with this spreadsheet and allow others to view it depending on what type of system you install.

One thing to always take into account when dealing with the computers is the threat of a security breach. There is always a possibility of computer abuse or misuse. Whether the misuse is intentional or not it stills needs to be addressed and prevented. The Computer Fraud and Abuse Act is a law passed by the United States Congress 1984 intended to reduce cracking or hacking of computer systems and to address federal computer-related offenses

Organizations commonly are required to assess and choose a range of information technology (IT) security services. These services are intended to regulate, maintain and advance their whole IT security program. It is complex and exigent to establish service contributor's capability, determine service dependability and navigate the complexity implicated in security service agreements. The six phases of the IT security life cycle are: initiation, assessment, solution, implementation, operations, and closeout (http://csrc.nist.gov/publications).

Attempting to addresses the issues affecting information a discussion of management and organizational issues that have a direct relationship to IT and local needs; a discussion of the problems in which this new program can solve development and deployment.

Bringing about an Information Technology plan gives rise to efficient tactic to target the changing technological requirements of the employees. First do background on the system you are thinking about using. Then evaluate it for cost or to see if it fits your needs. Then ask other staff to give their opinion. Do a budget analysis to see if you have enough money.

What factors can often overcome the IT security technologies that companies and individuals use to protect their information. The United States has laws that other countries do not have to deal with these sort of attacks such as defense strategy, firewall protection. A firewall is a protection that prevents computers from being accessed by unauthorized persons. It is just one layer of defense.

The person needs to set the firewall and still be mindful of sites they enter and activity on their computer. Some routers have protection on them, and some computer operating systems also have security and safety. It is best to activate all of the protection that is available to protect sensitive material.

There are ways to reach the goal of using technology in health care to improve population health outcomes. Health information technology is so important in improving health equity and quality of care. Disparities in access to health care information can affect how patients use new technology. Some barriers such as race, age, primary language, literacy skills, and vision and hearing may contribute to them seeing technology as complex and additional skills may be needed.

Organizations are benefitting from using technology by being able to streamline how they deliver their information to the patients, doctors, and other healthcare providers.

Clinicians are using more mobile devices at work. This mobile usage among nurses has doubled since 2012. Doctors are reporting that they are using their

Smart phones to do research quickly because it is portable when compared to a desktop PC. They also report that they use their Smartphone to make clinical calculations and interact with electronic medical records. Many health care facilities have an implemented bring your own device (BYOD) policies, ensuring that the Bluetooth discovery disabled, so their information is not easily compromised.

I would promote the usage of Smartphone and other mobile devices within the facility with restrictions on what type of information to be accessed. I would caution patients to be mindful of the Smartphone apps when trying to self-diagnose. I am concerned, however about what protections are put in place to protect sensitive, confidential health care data. Where does that information go when a patient loses their phone or trade it in for a new one? I would promote for patient usages for alerts, basic monitoring of results that they already keep such as blood glucose readings, weight, and fluid intake.

Using business computer for personal use

Employees, as well as organizations, may have a distorted notion of what boundaries are. Now with advancement in technology, it may be difficult to determine what is private information, and when has a company gone too far. Companies have innovative techniques of monitor employees' use of the internet. The rationale for this is to maximize employee productivity. Businesses have an obligation to themselves to protect their equipment that is used by employees and to maintain their integrity of the organization.

A company has the right to protect their shareholders and the community by monitoring the use of equipment by employees especially if that employee has access to sensitive material. Employees define invasion of privacy as a company having personal knowledge about them that would otherwise not be made public. People believe their behaviors outside of work, on their individual free time, are private and separate from their actions related to the company.

There are negatives associated with businesses monitoring their employee actions such as distrust among the business and its employees. Research indicates that "approximately 22.8 million U.S. employees waste one or more hours on the internet each day" (Black).

There will always be a discussion on what information employers should have access to and what should stay private. Organizations can also abuse this power, but they can hide behind the consideration that they own the office equipment and consequently have the authority to stipulate how it is used.

An employee should know better than to conduct private business using equipment of the company in the first place. Do not send private emails using your company issued email address. Use your personal cell phone or your personal email account. Some of these are just common sense. If it is their equipment, their property, then it is safe to assume that they own it. If the business has cause to suspect misuse of mobile devices, such as cell phones, and computers, the company has the right to protect against inappropriate behavior

Healthcare Center and Healthcare Cost

"Take 2 tablespoons of competition and call me in the morning." Sometimes competition is a reality check for all organizations. Healthcare is not an exception. People are beginning to realize that they have options when it comes to the care they receive.

My direct competition is larger health and wellness centers. However, I have an advantage because I am locally owned and managed. I live in the immediate area and have earned the trust of the community. They consider me their neighbor. They know that it is not just a job to me, but it is my brand and I do it with passion.

Any organization has no other choice but to give serious consideration to their competitors because it is the rival companies that influences the cost of services and good by competing for customers' demands. An organization has to identify strategies that make them stand out from the rest. The quality of service varies, but horizontal integration makes it possible for an organization to eliminating its competition by acquiring it.

Vertical integration eliminates two organizations from being reluctant to work together due to fear of one organization relinquishing more power to the other company. The customer can shop around to find a better deal just as a client or patient can shop around to find a more competitive priced health and wellness center.

Healthcare cost

The problem with health care is not health care; it is the delivery systems and the policies involved. The first thing that people want to do is to change or revised the policy. One of the reasons that people are upset about revising healthcare policies in the United States is a lack of understanding.

To properly address a policy change, the policy has to be fully understood. One understands the current healthcare system that we have; they are all money making gamblers who have no idea what is really happing. Some would argue that doctors and nurses understand healthcare but others think that they are just benefactors of the reaping the wealth.

I always ask my patients if their doctor really care about them and of course they all answer "yes." They believe that they do. Then I ask them if their nurses care about them or if they think I care about them, and they all answer "yes." Then I ask them about the big bad insurance company and they say, "Not a chance." So I ask them why they feel that the insurance company dislikes them whereas the doctors, nurse, healthcare providers including myself care do like them. They said that insurance companies just want their money and to become rich.

That is when the discussion begins. It is actually factual they the only industry that benefits from you being *sick* is healthcare that includes doctors, nurses, but not insurance companies. Only hospitals, doctors, get paid when you are SICK. Insurance companies want you to stay well so they do not have to pay your benefits claims. Therefore, they are actually on your side health wise. Not because of you but because of the money; but still.

Some believe that your doctor will tell you enough just to keep you alive and functioning, but your doctor has the key to getting you well and keep you well by educating you and not medicating you. Your doctor can tell you want you need to do never to have to suffer or die from a preventable disease like diabetes, heart disease, and high cholesterol. But wait then he will not make any money. Cost is very crucial and effect how I charge for services. All of these have to be considered as I manage my business.

Factors that shape healthcare policies are personal interest groups, politicians, the media, and small amounts of research who also has a financial interest to keep the grant money coming. And the uneducated patient is trapped in the middle. We can form all of these committees and groups that have not accomplished anything. The patient needs to become their own advocate.

Using the power of the media to influence health care politics. The media places more emphasis on a problem that is a concern to many, but they exacerbate the problem by the way they report it. Every commentary has an opinion about healthcare even if they have no idea how it is done.

Policy analyst role in the federal government is very influential and are seen as experts. The information they used is supposed to be based on researched information and not their personal opinion and alternatives. The analyst is more of a bureaucrat than an expert.

The role of a health care policy analyst is to assist and incorporate health concerns during the implementation of new policies, services, and plans. The information gathered by the analyst is intended to improve awareness and understanding of the existing health care concerns and challenges. They must be able to analyze and interpret community health data. Some participation in the community to gather and listen to the thoughts and concerns of everyday citizens, and relay those concerns to stakeholders as an attempt to ensure connectivity between input of the community, government officials and public.

The concerns and needs of the public should be a priority of the healthcare analyst when developing a policy option for decision makers. They should make sure that the information is factual, confidential and unbiased.

During some research, I found out that the United States spends 17 percent of its gross domestic product (GDP) on health care, by far the most of any nation in the world. Moreover, the rate of health care spending is rapidly outstripping the rate of growth of our economy, so that by 2080 health care spending is projected to account for 40 percent of the U.S. economy (CBO, 2010a). Despite this high level of spending, there remain enormous disparities in access to health care in our nation.

The CBO estimates that exchange premiums will be 10–13 percent higher, on average, with reform than in the non-group market absent reform although for any family below 400 percent of poverty this cost could be partially offset by tax credits(CBO, 2010). CBO also estimates that the revenue increases and spending cuts will exceed the new level of spending, reducing the federal deficit by more than $100 billion in the first decade and more than $1 trillion in the second decade.

The rate of growth in health care spending in the U.S. has outpaced the growth rate in the gross domestic product (GDP), inflation, and population for many years. Official price a hospital or doctor charges for a service is rarely the amount that hospital or doctor expects to be paid, and what will be paid varies enormously, depending on which private insurance a patient has, or whether one of the big government programs, Medicare or Medicaid, acts as the insurer. This part of managing a business can become time-consuming so you may want to hire a specific person to handle the billing and coding.

Hospitals, of course, are labor intensive places with enormous costs in personnel and equipment. They lose money on treatments for uninsured people who cannot or will not pay their bills. According to some analysts, they also lose on Medicare and Medicaid, the programs for elderly and poor people, and some of that loss is made up from the higher charges paid by private insurance companies.

A recent study showed that private insurance companies paid 41 % more to hospitals and 23 %

more to individual doctors than Medicare paid for the same procedures. Medicare gets to dictate the price.

Health Insurance Exchange also known as The Health Care Market Place, is basic economics. An exchange is as pro-market a mechanism as they come: free up buyers and sellers, standardize the products, and add pricing transparency. State-organized marketplaces where non-group and small group insurers must compete in a transparent marketplace that is designed to maximize competition and lower premiums.

Soon the cost should level out: The Patient Protection and Affordable Care Act (ACA), signed into law on March 23, 2010, by President Obama is the most comprehensive reform of the U.S. medical system in at least 45 years.

Health and Wellness Communication

The heart and art of medicine are doctor-patient communication. Effective communication between a care provider and patient is very important in delivering high- quality health care. The breakdown in communication is on the top of the list of patient dissatisfaction and complaints.

I believe that web-based communication on health issues is a viable approach to improving patient-doctor relationships. It can improve communications, and practice efficiency. Some of the barriers are some people are still not that tech savvy and fear the internet. A web site set up to facilitate communication between a doctor and his patient is convenient for the patient and it removes the time and distance restraints that many patient may have with transportation issues getting back and forth to their doctor's office.

Web-based communication will benefit those patients who want an immediate look at their records, test results, and on-line medication refills. The groups of patients that benefit the most are those who are very involved with their health and those who have internet access. The language barrier would have to be address as well as the cultural differences that may preclude Spanish speaking population from being interested in the web-based interaction with their physician.

Some of the benefits to on-line patient doctor communication is that the patient does not have to call into the doctor's office and get placed on hold waiting to speak to the doctor. This method also frees up the staff. The doctor does not have to leave a patient's room to come to the phone, and there is a reduction in telephone wait on-hold time. The doctor does not have to waste time telling the nurse what to tell the patient. Instead, he can just email or tell the patient himself.

Some organizations have the technology that allow a patient to fill out the pre-registration form and pre-op check lists over the internet, reducing the time it takes to fill in those form once in the facility.

Some of the major concerns that come to mind is security and privacy. Whenever there is an advancement in technology, there comes along with it a security risk. Some people are concerned that their medical information can be easily accessed by strangers or computer hackers.

Convenience is the biggest selling point to web-based patient-doctor communication because we live in a society that is always on the go, multitasking and wants things instantly.

What is Electronic Medical Records (EMR)

Electronic medical records (EMR) are a computer digital version of a patient's records that was once a paper version. The chart still contains pertinent health information such as a patient's medical history, current diagnosis and current laboratory and diagnostic test. Most EMR are used by clinicians to diagnose and treat.

The most important purpose of the medical record is to provide a place of storage of the health care provider's observations, analysis, and treatment of the patient. Most patient-clinician interactions begin with the chief complaint: "What brings you here today?" Once the clinicians objectively document the patient's complaint, perform a physical exam, and then a brief history is obtained from the patient or family member if the patient is unable to speak. A patient's medical record will contain the present patient illness, the history of symptoms that are related, past medical history, family history and some social and behavioral history.

Electronic medical records can track that information over time. The EMR can to be utilized by the appropriate person who needs to access it at any time whether they are in a clinic across town, in a remote area, or across the continent. EMR help immediately identifies patients, monitor their health progression, keep track of scheduled vaccinations and laboratory testing, and improve overall healthcare. EMR are convenient, and it defies the barrier of the invisible wall of time and distance, but it is not without challenges and obstacles.

Problems challenges of Electronic Medical Records. Organizational challenges to Electronic Medical Records are the startup cost. Studies have proven that having an EMR system saves time and money in the long run, but the initial cost may be a burden for some facilities. Other concerns include computer down-time, lack of standards, and increased provider time.

Providers are concerned that they are spending far too much time keying information into the computer and are not spending quality time with their patients. Some providers complain that they do not have access to the facility to obtain the records and in some cases the records have to be printed off and sent to the provider.

Some of the concerns of having or employing an Electronic Medical Records System include concerns for safety, privacy and confidentiality. Employing an EMR system creates with it its own vulnerability.

There may be hackers that know how to get pass security and ultimately access sensitive patient personal information.

Security Solutions for Electronic Medical Records. With appropriate security measure installed, an organization can benefit from having and Electronic Medical Records System. Organization implement policies and procedures that include signing a confidentially agreement stating understanding of patient privacy procedures. Most companies have security measures in place that trace whose accessing such records or at least leave a trail of individuals who accessed them. Often time employees are given passwords that are exclusive to them and give them access to sensitive, confidential patient information. In these situations, it is not likely that information will be breached or misused. Another concern with EMR is computer down- time and loss of data. Most institutions have suitable back-up systems that ensure and prevent permanent loss of patient's medical record.

They are computer protection software as well as hardware that can be put in place to layer security to patient's confidential medical records such as the firewall. A firewall as a "system or group of systems that enforces an access-control policy between two networks" (2011).

Firewalls are configured only to allow specific types of traffic in and out of the network. Firewalls cannot protect against unknown virus or malware threats and therefore require continuous updating. Effectiveness is entirely dependent on configuration. Firewalls cannot protect against traffic that does not pass through them, such as wireless and instant message traffic, as well as hand carried personal storage devices that may be attached to the network by an authorized user.

Firewalls cannot protect against intentional or unintentional security breaches by authorized network users, but nothing can protect from an experienced hacker. These measures are just put into place for prevention and deterrence, to prevent errors, deter criminals, deny access to unauthorized users, to find it before it is an issue.

The appropriate patient-provider communication should include providing the patient with access to their personal health information. This health information should include the patient's diagnosis, and treatment. There are so many health disparities that impede the effectiveness of the communication process. Some of those disparities and barriers are culture, ethnicity, race, gender, income, education, geographic location, sexual orientation, disability status, and other inequities such as speech, and cognitive disabilities.

There are more than 47 million people in America with limited English proficiency. This number does not just include foreign-born Americans or immigrants. There are a number of Americans, 90 million that have limited understanding and comprehension of the English language concerning medical and health literacy issues.

There are more than 30 million Americans living with deafness, hearing impairments. There is a population that has become impaired due to a recent illness such as a stroke, or accident. Other has speech impairment due to being sedated or having a breathing tube in their throat for breathing. These disparities can cause delay in medical treatment, increased healthcare cost, and poor patient outcomes and satisfaction.

Solutions after carefully identifying each patient communication needs the facility will implement assistant to facilitate two-way communications between the patient and his provider in ways that are convenient and meets the patient's need.

Change the way of thinking from the individual that have the deficient but to our communication strategies have the deficiencies for it takes more than words to communicate.

Use this as an opportunity to collaborate with other staff members, research material, colleagues and compliance offers. Establish with the admissions office the key questions to assess the patient on arrival to elicit and determine literacy and language need, cultural differences, and sensory impairments. Use this as an opportunity to implement training on communication, cultural and health literacy programs. Determine what needs to be included in the communication care plan as separate or as part of the regular care plan.

Implement language lines and speaking, and hearing assistive devices such as glasses, qualified language interpreter, hearing aids called pocket talker which amplifies sounds, speech-language pathologist, and communication vidatek boards.

- o Offer on-line communication such as email web based portals
- o Use adapted call switch or bells for notifying staff of needs

Many patients report that these new communication tools are more effective than the previous modes of communication such as the face-to-face visit or the telephone. The telephone was frustrating because of the navigation of what number to press and the hold or wait times left patients feeling as if they were getting the runaround.

For many patients, using online communication is much improved. Make sure that patient is allowed to have support from family and friend around to help them feel safe and more comfortable.

Reevaluate for progress and need for change and determine cost assignment. Participate in the outcome assessment and quality control. Establish if this new change will be included in or if it is added to the bill as an extra charge. Determine how the devices used are going to be disposed of. For example are the communication boards disposable of will they need cleaning? Contact the infection control department to collaborate with which equipment is single patient use, disposable or reusable.

Managing a business is America is rewarding. Being an entrepreneur should make you feel good knowing that you are a part of inventing, creating, or developing something new. I hope that I can be used as a role model to inspire, and foster a future entrepreneur whose challenges are similar to the ones I faced. Be prepared for setbacks and disappointments and understand that failure can be used as a learning experience.

Starting a new business checklist

- o Formulate an idea for a business
- o Choose a name for your business
- o Consider business cards, logo, website
- o Think about trademark business name
- o Seek assistance and business training
- o Write a business plan
- o Think about marketing strategy
- o Choose a business location
- o Seek funding and financing
- o Select an accountant or attorney
- o Obtain licensure and zoning permits
- o Obtain business insurance or bonding
- o Seek accreditation if necessary
- o Register a business name & obtain a DBA (Doing Business As)
- o Get a Tax ID number or EIN (Employer ID)

References & Suggested reading

Akin, M. (2011). Predicting Consumers' Behavioral Intentions with Perceptions of Brand Personality: A Study in Cell Phone Markets. *International Journal Of Business & Management*, 6(6), 193-206.

Black, Suzzane. IT Ethics. January 25, 2013. https://prezi.com/ro_a-ngmh7h4/it-ethics/

Bruche, M. (2011). Creditor Coordination, Liquidation Timing, and Debt Valuation. *Journal Of Financial & Quantitative Analysis*, 1407-1436.

Chief Executive.Net http://chiefexecutive.net/lists-rankings/

Congressional Budget Office, 2010a. *The Long-Term Budget Outlook.* Congressional Budget Office, Washington, DC

Department of Health and Human Service. National Action Plan to Improve

hhtp://www.health.gov/communication?HLActionPla
n

Gitman, L. J. (2012). *Principles of Mangerial Finance.* Prentice Hall.

Hanson, S., & Lee, B. (2013). U.S.-Cuba Relations. *Council on Foreign Relations.* Retrieved March 23, 2013, from www.cfr.org

Hughes, R. L. (2005). *Leadership: Enhancing the Lessons of Experience.* Richard D. Irwin, Inc.

The Joint Commission New Standard www.jointcommission.org

Keller, S. (2012). U.S. Export Laws and Related Trade Sanctions — The Harvard Law School Forum on Corporate Governance and Financial Regulation. *The Harvard Law School Forum on Corporate Governance and Financial Regulation.* Retrieved March 19, 2013, from http://blogs.law.harvard.edu/corpgov/2012/11/17/u-s-export-laws-and-related-trade

Kotler, P. &. (2011). Marketing Management 14 th edition. Pearson Prentice Hall.

Lee, S. Y. (2015, January 29). *Samsung Elec's Smartphone primacy under threat from Apple after weak Q4.* Retrieved from Reuters: http://www.reuters.com/article/2015/01/29/us-

samsung-elec-results-
idUSKBN0L12SO20150129

McDonald, D. (September 30, 2014). *The Firm: The Story of McKinsey and Its Secret Influence on American Business.* Simon & Schuster; Reprint edition.

Olajidetalabi, F., Chile, S., & Abubakri, O. (2012). Making Slogans and Unique Selling Propositions (USP) Beneficial to Advertisers and the Consumers. *New Media & Mass Communication*

Taylor, C. R. (n.d.). The Impact of Brand Differentiating Messages on the Effectiveness of Korean Advertising. *Journal Of International Marketing*, 2(4), 31-52.

Takeyh, R. (2013). What should U.S. policy toward Iran be in order to prevent further development of its nuclear program?. *Council on Foreign Relations.* Retrieved March 23, 2013, from: http://www.cfr.org/iran/should-us-policy-toward-iran-order-prevent- further-development-its-nuclear-program/p30244

U.S. Department of the Treasury. (2013). Terrorism and Financial Intelligence. *Office of Foreign Assets*

Control (OFAC). Retrieved March 19, 2013, from
www.treasury.gov

UN Sanctions against Iran. (2013). Retrieved from
Global Policy Forum:
http://www.globalpolicy.org/security-council/index-
of-countries-on-the-security-council-
agenda/iran.html

Wang, G., Dou, W., Li, H., & Zhou, N. (2013).
Advertiser Risk Taking, Campaign Originality,
and Campaign Performance. *Journal Of
Advertising, 42*(1), 42-53

Wild, J. J. & Wild, K. L. (2012). *International
Business: The Challenges of Globalization* (6th ed.).
Upper Saddle River, NJ: Pearson Prentice Hall

http://www.health.gov/healthliteracyonline/why.htm

http://www.businessinsider.com/ten-billionaires-
give-you-the-best-investment-advice-they-know-
2011-11?op=1#ixzz2M7jWyxGL

rowing a business from the start of a vision to finished product through trategic business planning, innovative sales techniques, and pioneering narketing design. Knowledge and skilled in all aspects of the healthcare ustry including direct patient care, Long Term Care, Insurance & Billing ough years successes , failures & tears using what I have learned and is still learning.

Business Management in America

My entrepreneurial perspective

BY: Tonya B. Hunter

www.ingramcontent.com/pod-product-compliance
Lightning Source LLC
Chambersburg PA
CBHW021435170526
45164CB00001B/250